FREEDOM

Freedom from:

Generational Curses

Word Curses/Judgments

Ungodly Soul-Ties

Spirit of Offense

Spirit of Rejection

Plus

Setting Your Boundaries

Warfare Prayers

Little Sparrow Ministries

Copyright @ 2017 by Little Sparrow Ministries, Revised 2021
All Rights Reserved
Printed in the United States of America
International Standard Book Number:
978-1-4951-6835-2

**Little Sparrow Ministries
PO Box 307
Lindale, Texas 75771
Email: lsparrowministries@gmail.com
Web site:
www.littlesparrowministries.com**

Co-authored:
    Our Lord and Savior, Jesus Christ
    Judy H. Farris-Smith

Scripture quotations marked (NIV) are taken from the HOLY BIBLE, NEW INTERNATIONAL VERSION®. NIV®. Copyright © 1973, 1978, 1984 by International Bible Society. Used by permission of Zondervan. All rights reserved.

No part of this book may be reproduced or transmitted in any form or by any means, electronic or mechanical, including photocopying, recording, or by any information storage and retrieval system, without permission in writing from Little Sparrow Ministries.

INGRAM BOOK DISTRIBUTOR

Introduction
FREEDOM

When God's Truth comes forth in our beliefs, confessions, renouncements, and forgiveness, we are set free from Satan's chains.

John 8:32 NIV Then you will know the truth, and the truth will set you free.

The word also states, "My people are destroyed from lack of knowledge." *Hosea 4:6 NIV*

In this book, I am giving you knowledge to break some of Satan's chains and to begin the process of setting you free. You are not a victim; you live in victory.

Please read out loud all the prayers in this book. Satan cannot read your mind.

Judy H. Farris-Smith

Table of Contents

Generational Curses 1
    Prayers 11

Word Curses/Judgments 28
    Prayers 36

Ungodly Soul-ties 40
    Prayers 41

Spirit of Offense 44
    Prayer 57

Spirit of Rejection 59
    Prayers 64

Setting Your Boundaries 69
    Prayer 83

Warfare Prayers 85

Books and References Studied 88

Other Books by the Author 92

Current/Generational Curses

My people are destroyed from lack of knowledge. Hosea 4:6

Does your family have continuous problems with: poverty, barrenness, depression, anger, rebellion, catastrophic accidents, mental illness, suicides, addictions, divorce, abuse, sexual sins, sicknesses such as cancer, and heart disease? The list could go on and on.

Are you a Christian that attends church regularly and does everything possible to lead a godly life? Are you still plagued by the above problems and more? The answer could be curses that have been allowed on your family line because of:

1. Generational sins
2. Involvement in the occult
3. Negative spoken words
4. Personal sins which open doors
5. Ungodly soul-ties from other individuals and groups

As a result of the above, curses may have been allowed on your ancestors, you, and your family by:

- God
- Satan having a legal right to curse
- Satan and demonic spirits that do not have a legal right to curse

1. Generational Sins

Research your family's history; determine if the same problems are passed down from one generation to the next. If so, that is called a generational curse. Can you see a pattern?

Through conception, weaknesses and behavioral tendencies are passed down to us because of inheriting the iniquities of our fathers. Thereby, the curses are passed on to each successive generation as they commit the same sins.

Lamentations 5:7 NIV Our fathers sinned and are no more, and we bear their punishment.

Numbers 14:18 NIV The Lord is slow to anger, abounding in love and forgiving sin and rebellion. Yet he does not leave the guilty unpunished; he punishes the children for the sins of the fathers to the third and fourth generations.

Jeremiah 15:13 NIV Your wealth and your treasures I will give as plunder, without charge, because of all your sins throughout your country.

Jeremiah 6:19 NIV Hear O earth: I am bringing disaster on this people, the fruit of their schemes, because they have not listened to my words and have rejected my law.

We are responsible for our own actions and lack of knowledge does not excuse us from knowing the truth. God still holds us accountable. Therefore, we must read and understand God's word.

Leviticus 5:17 NIV If a person sins and does what is forbidden in any of the Lord's commands, even though he does not know it, he is guilty and will be held responsible.

The key to preventing generational curses is consistent repentance for our sins, known and unknown. We must ask God to cleanse us, set us free, and change our behavior. The Holy Spirit will direct and guide us if we only ask him.

Isaiah 5:13 NIV Therefore my people will go into exile for lack of understanding; their men of rank will die of hunger and their masses will be parched with thirst.

2. Involvement in the occult

Curses can be derived from your involvement in the occult or from other people that have been under Satan's authority.

3. Negative spoken words

We must scrutinize our vocabulary. *Matthew 12:37 NIV* For by your words you will be acquitted, and by your words you will be condemned.

4. Personal sins

The key is consistent repentance for your sins and living according to God's truths.

5. Ungodly soul-ties

Be aware of soul-ties of the past and the soul-ties that are created by you in the future.

Curses allowed by God

In the seventh chapter of Joshua, Israel sinned against God; and as a result, thirty-six of its men perished.

Joshua 7:1 NIV But the Israelites acted unfaithfully in regard to the devoted things; Achan son of Carmi, the son of Zimri, the son of Zerah, of the tribe of Judah, took some of them. So, the Lord's anger burned against Israel.

The children of Israel were cursed by God many times because of their unrepentant sins and disobedience.

Curses placed by Satan who has a legal right.

If we knowingly or unknowingly have sinned, we can cause a door to open for Satan and his demonic spirits legally to enter.

God does not destroy or bring calamity upon us, but he does allow Satan at times to do so.

Curses placed by Satan who does not have a legal right.

Because we are Christians who are walking righteously with the Lord, Satan will send tormenting spirits in various forms to harass, discourage, defile, deceive, compel, enslave, and to cause fear, and sickness. God has given us the power and authority to bind the strongmen and their demonic spirits and to rebuke their actions.

If you have children, please read the following before proceeding any further.

We recommend that you and your children pray through, ***Set Yourself Free Little Children and Come to Me***. This is an easy-to-read non-threatening booklet for your children.

From our understanding of the scriptures, the age of twelve could be considered the age of accountability. Parents cannot break generational curses off anyone except their own very small children.

At the age of twelve, each person is accountable for their own actions;

they must break the generational curses off themselves. If you have small children and when you pray the breaking prayers, insert your children's names in the appropriate places.

Prayers for Breaking Generational Curses

Ask the Holy Spirit to show you what curses have been placed on you and your ancestors. To break curses allowed by God, Satan who has a legal right, and Satan, who does not have a legal right, please pray the following prayers out loud in the order indicated:

Prayer for Breaking Curses Allowed By God

Heavenly Father,

Heavenly Father, I come to you in the name of our Lord Jesus Christ and by virtue of his shed blood, I ask you to forgive me of my sins and the sins of my forefathers, those that are known and are not known.

Lord, I ask that you remove and completely destroy all the roots and seeds of my own personal sins and my ancestors' sins. Lord, I ask that you transfuse my blood line with yours; thereby, eliminating anything unholy to a blood line of purity and holiness. I ask you to shut my bloodline doors that have been opened because of curses.

I ask you to separate me (and my children) from the generational curse or curses that you have allowed on my life because of the sins of my forefathers or my own personal sins. I declare and decree that it is done. Thank you, Lord. Amen.

Prayer for Breaking Curses from Satan Having Legal Authority

The book, ***Setting Yourself Free, Deliverance from Darkness***, teaches about the sixteen biblically based strongmen that may have gained strongholds over different areas of your life.

Heavenly Father,

By the authority and power given to me by the holy name of our Lord, Jesus Christ, I bind, break the soul-ties, break your power, and cast off me (and my children) the strongmen of spirit of divination, familiar spirit, spirit of jealousy, lying spirit, perverse spirit, spirit of haughtiness, spirit of heaviness, spirit of whoredoms, spirit of infirmity, dumb and deaf spirit, spirit of bondage, spirit of fear, seducing spirits, spirit of anti-Christ, spirit of error, spirit of death, and all other demonic spirits that were associated with all generational curses which include familiar spirits, familial spirits, and dormant spirits. Lord, I ask you to shut all my bloodline doors that have been opened due to Satan having legal authority.

I demand that you separate from me now as you have no legal right to stay. Go to the arid places, and never return. Holy Spirit please come and fill the void places within me. I declare and decree that it is done. Amen.

Satan and Demonic Spirits That Do Not Have a Legal Right to Curse

Before doing this prayer, you will need to do some research into your family line. Find the negative occurrences in your family line. A few examples are torment, divorce, abortion, poverty, anger, offense, rejection, mental problems, negative thoughts, cancer, and arthritis. Make a list.

In the next prayer, you will use your authority given to you by our Lord, Jesus Christ. Please insert the names of any demonic spirits that have tormented and harassed you and your ancestors. Take them from your list.

Heavenly Father,

By the authority and power given to me by the holy name of our Lord, Jesus Christ, I demand these curses of _____ (e.g., poverty, cancer, anger) to be broken now and forever more. Lord, I ask you to shut all the bloodline doors that have been opened because of generational curses.

I bind, break the soul-ties, break your power, and cast out of me (and my children) all demonic spirits, familiar spirits, familial spirits, and dormant spirits that were associated with these curses.

I demand you to separate from me (and my children) now as you have no legal right to stay. Go to the arid places, and never return. Holy Spirit please come and fill the void places within me. I declare and decree that it is done. Amen

Other wrongful behaviors may have gained a stronghold in your life. It could be because of your sins or the sins of your ancestors. No matter what the reason, you now have the tools to break these curses and change your behavior.

To prevent future ancestral curses, you must repent if you have sinned. You must change your behavior and walk in truth and righteousness.

GENERATIONAL CURSES AS A RESULT OF MULTI-RACIAL SLAVERY

According to the Britannica Online Encyclopedia, the definition of a slave is:

"Slavery is the condition in which one human being was owned by another. A slave was considered as property or chattel and was deprived of most of the rights ordinarily held by free persons.

"It was a form of dependent labor performed by a nonfamily member. The slave was deprived of personal liberty and the right to move about geographically as he desired.

"Slaves were generated in many ways. Probably the most frequent was capture in war. Others were kidnapped on slave-raiding or piracy expeditions. Many slaves were the offspring of slaves. Some people were enslaved as a punishment for crime or debt; others were sold into slavery by their parents, other relatives, or even spouses, sometimes to satisfy debts, sometimes to escape starvation.

"Slavery existed almost everywhere throughout history. It seems to have been especially important in the development of two of the world's major civilizations, Western (including ancient Greece and Rome) and Islamic societies."

There have been two basic types of slavery throughout recorded history. The first is domestic or household slavery, and the second is productive slavery. The first type is self-explanatory; however, the second type was to produce marketable commodities in mines or on plantations.

Slave ownership has existed and, in some cases, still exists in the following countries: China, Korea, Greece, Rome, India, Thailand, Burma, Philippines, Nepal, Malaya, Pakistan, Turkey, Egypt, Indonesia, Japan, Africa, and Islamic people worldwide.

The American Indians, Incas, Mayans, Aztecs, England, Scandinavia, France, Germany, Poland, Lithuania, Russia, and America also had slave societies. This list is not all inclusive.

People from all races became slaves. In fact, there were white slaves in America before there were black slaves.

According to historian, Michael A Hoffman, "Up to one-half of all the arrivals in the American colonies were white slaves, and they were America's first slaves. These whites were slaves for life, long before blacks ever were.

"This slavery was even hereditary. White children born to white slaves were enslaved too. Nine-tenths of the white slavery in America was conducted without indentures of any kind but according to the so-called 'custom of the country,' as it was known, which was lifetime slavery, administered by the white slave merchants themselves. There were also black slave merchants who owned white slaves."

Historian, Oscar Handlin, writes that in colonial America, "White servants (slaves) could be bartered for profit, sold to the highest bidder for the unpaid debts of their masters, and otherwise transferred like movable goods or chattels.

"The condition of the first Negroes in the continental English colonies must be viewed within the perspective of these conceptions and realities of white servitude." In 1789, thousands of Irish slaves, children and adults were sold to America and Australia.

According to historian, Robert Davis, "Between, 1530 and 1780 there were almost certainly 1 million and quite possibly as many as 1.25 million white, European Christians enslaved by the Muslims of the Barbary Coast. Slaves were still slaves whether they are black or white, and whether they suffered in America or North Africa."

According to the online Wikipedia, "The treatment of slaves in the United States varied by time and place but was generally brutal and degrading. Whipping, execution, and sexual abuse including rape were common.

"Slaves were punished by whipping, shackling, hanging, beating, burning, mutilation, branding, and/or imprisonment. Punishment was most often meted out in response to disobedience or perceived infractions, but slaves were also sometimes abused to assert the dominance of their master or overseer. The mistreatment of slaves frequently included rape, and the sexual abuse of women. Many slaves were killed because of resisting sexual attacks. Others sustained psychological and physical trauma."

We must, therefore, conclude that a great percentage of our population, probably have had an ancestor that had been a slave. Because of this, we may have inherited behavior characteristics or curses.

Because of these harsh treatments, doors were opened that

allowed demonic forces to enter in our mind, spirit, and body. It is necessary to close these doors. Please pray out loud the following prayer:

Heavenly Father,

I come to you in the name of our Lord, Jesus Christ, and by virtue of his shed blood. I ask you to cleanse me and destroy all the demonic ancestral roots and seeds that are the result of the life of slavery.

I know that there were sins committed by my ancestors as result of being in servitude. Some of these sins were: rebellion, murder, alcoholism, suicide, arson, rape, lethargy (refusing to work), sluggishness, passivity, and indifference. I realize that most of this behavior was the result of over control by their masters, and the absence of freedom.

I ask you to separate me (and my children) from the generational curses and demonic inherited behaviors that have been allowed on my life because of my forefathers' sins. Lord, I ask you to shut all my bloodline doors that have been opened due to slavery. Lord, I ask that you transfuse my bloodline with yours; thereby, eliminating anything unholy to a blood line of purity and holiness.

I prophetically decree that my mind, my body, and my spirit are totally set free from the ancestral curses and demonically inherited behavior characteristics that have occurred because of my ancestors' slavery. I declare and decree that it is done! Amen.

Word Curses, Judgments, and Speaking Positively

1 Peter 3:10 NIV For, whoever would love life and see good days must keep his tongue from evil and his lips from deceitful speech.

Matthew 12:34-37 NIV …for out of the overflow of the heart the mouth speaks. The good man brings good things out of the good stored up in him, and the evil man brings evil things out of the evil stored up in him. But I tell you that men will have to give account on the Day of Judgment for every careless word they have spoken. For by your words, you will be acquitted, and by your words you will be condemned.

James 3:9-10 NIV With the tongue we praise our Lord and Father and with it we curse men, who have been made in God's likeness. Out of the same mouth come praise and cursing. My brothers, this should not be.

Psalm 52:2-4 NIV Your tongue plots destruction; it is like a sharpened razor, you who practice deceit. You love evil rather than good and falsehood rather than speaking the truth. You love every harmful word, O you deceitful tongue!

Proverbs 12:18 NIV Reckless words pierce like a sword, but the tongue of the wise brings healing.

Proverbs 10:18-21 NIV He who conceals his hatred has lying lips, and whoever spreads slander is a fool. When words are many, sin is not absent, but he who holds his tongue is wise. The tongue of the righteous is choice silver, but the heart of the wicked is of little value. The lips of the righteous nourish many, but fools die for lack of judgment.

1 Corinthians 4:12-13 NIV …When we are cursed, we bless; when we are persecuted, we endure it; when we are slandered, we answer kindly.

Deuteronomy 30:7 NIV The Lord your God will put all these curses on your enemies who hate and persecute you.

Luke 6:28 NIV Bless those who curse you, pray for those who mistreat you.

Word Curses

Negative words are harmful. Casual and/or destructive remarks often become self-fulfilling prophecies.

We can easily internalize destructive words. This internalization can govern our future behavior because our behavior or actions usually follow spoken words. As a result, Satan has gained a foothold in our lives by establishing a seedbed of lies.

Wrongful prayers, gossip, and slander are examples of word curses. Prayers that try to control and manipulate someone according to another's fleshly desires are an abomination to God.

The sin of murder is committed when one gossips or slanders another.

They not only can kill a person's reputation but also can physically harm them.

Note: In order to see the hand of God work in our lives, we must forgive those who have harmed us. Do not let a root of bitterness develop.

Judgments

Judge: to make up one's mind about; form an opinion or estimate about; to think; suppose; conclude; to criticize; blame; and condemn. Judgment: a decision; decree; a decision made by anybody who judges; a misfortune thought of as a punishment from God. (*The World Book Dictionary 1981 Edition.*)

Romans 14:10 NIV You, then, why do you judge your brother? Or why do you look down on your brother? For we all stand before God's judgment seat.

James 2:13 NIV …because judgment without mercy will be shown to anyone who has not been merciful. Mercy triumphs over judgment.

Lamentations 5:7 NIV Our fathers sinned and are no more, and we bear their punishment.

Luke 6:37 NIV Do not judge, and you will not be judged. Do not condemn, and you will not be condemned. Forgive, and you will be forgiven.

If we scrutinize our vocabulary, we can determine where we are spiritually. Are we bringing God's truth into the world by speaking positively or are we bringing in the enemy's darkness by speaking negatively?

Our behaviors or actions usually follow our spoken words, and our spoken words reveal the true condition of our hearts. As we speak positive and edifying words, we confirm the word of God in our lives and in others.

Psalm 12:6 NIV And the words of the Lord are flawless, like silver, refined in a furnace of clay, purified seven times.

Psalm 33:6 NIV By the word of the Lord were the heavens made; their starry host by the breath of his mouth.

Matthew 8:8 NIV The centurion replied, "Lord, I do not deserve to have you come under my roof. But just say the word, and my servant will be healed." *(The centurion had faith in the power of the spoken word of Jesus.)*

Matthew 17:20 NIV He replied, "Because you have so little faith, I tell you the truth, if you have faith as small as a mustard seed, you can say to this mountain, 'Move from here to there' and it will move. Nothing will be impossible for you." *(He said just speak to those things that are not as though they were.)*

Mark 11:23 NIV I tell you the truth, if anyone says to this mountain, "Go throw yourself into the sea," and does not doubt in his heart but believes that what he says will happen, it will be done for him.

John 15:7-8 NIV If you remain in me and my words remain in you, ask whatever you wish, and it will be given you. This is to my Father's glory, that you bear much fruit, showing yourselves to be my disciples.

Prayer for Breaking Word Curses/ Judgments

Heavenly Father,

By the authority and power given to me by the holy name of our Lord, Jesus Christ, I demand all word curses, judgments, and assignments, and all curses from witchcraft, jealousy, envy, and strife are broken and shattered; I demand they are separated from me now. Lord, I ask you to shut all my bloodline doors that have been opened due to word curses and judgments.

I demand that all strongmen and demonic spirits that are associated with these curses to separate from me now. Go to the arid places, and never return. In the name of Jesus, I ask you to send blessings and conviction to the originator.

Holy Spirit, I ask you to come and fill all the void places within me. I declare and decree that it is done! Amen.

I personally use the above prayer on a regular basis. I stay away from gossiping people and try to scrutinize my words daily. Curses can harm us physically, spiritually, and emotionally.

Prayer for Speaking Positively

Heavenly Father,

In the name of Jesus, I ask for ears to hear, eyes to see, and a mouth that speaks spiritual truths. I ask that your truths penetrate my innermost being, so my words are always positive and edifying. I ask for a new mind-set so that my thoughts, attitudes, and actions are always positive even in the middle of difficult or dark circumstances.

I prophetically decree that from this day forth I will speak blessings over myself and others, and that I will speak to those things that are not as though they were.

Please help me, Lord, by opening my natural eyes to see the impact my positive and edifying words have over my life and the lives of others.

Lord, I ask that you take me to a new level of faith and spiritual maturity. I declare and decree that it is done! Amen.

Ungodly Soul-Ties

A soul-tie can be described as the linking together of two individuals, i.e., becoming one in their souls. God designed a soul-tie as a two-way interaction for the flow of love between two parties. Godly soul-ties are created between friends and family members.

Ungodly soul-ties are created between individuals because of sins. If relationships are based on dependence, bondage or idolatry, an unhealthy soul-tie has developed. Also, relationships can become ungodly because of adultery, manipulation, control, or co-dependency. An ungodly soul-tie can develop between you and a substance that develops into an addiction.

Please destroy all pictures or personal items belonging to anyone with whom you have an ungodly soul-tie.

Prayer to Break Ungodly Soul-Ties

Heavenly Father,

In the name of Jesus, I break the ungodly soul-tie with _____ (name).

I ask that you cleanse me from all unrighteousness because of any known or unknown agreement that resulted in an ungodly soul-tie.

I ask that you sever all strongholds that have formed because of this ungodly action. Forgive me, Lord, for my part in creating this ungodly soul-tie.

I also ask you to heal my emotions and to assemble and heal all the fragmented pieces of my soul. I decree that my soul has been restored. I plead the blood of Christ over my spirit, soul, and body. I declare and decree that it is done! Amen.

Prayer to Break Godly Soul-ties

To break the soul-tie with the deceased, divorced, or abandoned spouse, parent, or friend, pray the following prayer:

Heavenly Father,

In the name of Jesus, I break the soul-tie with _____(name).

I ask you, Lord, to heal my emotions, to assemble, and to heal all the fragmented pieces of my soul. I decree that my soul has been restored. I plead the blood of Christ over my spirit, soul, and body. Lord, I ask that you transfuse my bloodline with yours; thereby, eliminating anything unholy to a bloodline of purity and holiness. I decree and declare that it is done! Amen.

There may be situations where family members are heavily involved in the occult or other sins. These sins could be affecting you or your family adversely. If this is the case, sever the soul-tie. Children may need to break soul-ties for them to move on with their lives.

Spirit of Offense

Forgiveness is truly at the heart of God. God sees us through his eyes of love. "Lord, please allow us to see through your eyes."

We cannot live in this world without becoming offended. So, we must prepare for this deadly trap of Satan's – the spirit of offense. We do not want demonic strongholds in our lives. It would stop God's plans for us and our sensitivity to him.

Our lives are based on relationships. With spiritual laws and truths, the Word of God shows each of us how to live Godly lives. God is concerned with our behavior. Does our behavior reflect His love, kindness, gentleness, compassion, and mercy?

In *Matthew 24*, one of the signs of his impending return is "many will be offended". He will demand agape love from us – unconditional love.

Sometimes we may offend others knowingly or unknowingly. The reverse can also happen, and we can become offended or wronged. Then do we ACT with Godly wisdom or REACT in an ungodly manner.

There are three categories of wrongs or offenses:

1. Offenses you have committed. You must go immediately to the individual and ask for forgiveness.

2. Offenses that have been committed against you.

3. Offenses that you have perceived have been committed against you but were not.

A reaction to an offense can be hurt, disappointment, frustration, anger, and resentment.

Only those you care about can hurt you. You expect more from them. After all, you have given more of yourself to them. The more severe offenses are caused by close relationships. We expect these behaviors in the world and not in our churches. Many people in the church become wounded, hurt, and bitter.

When we become offended or wronged, the enemy will try to keep the offense hidden and surrounded in pride. Pride will keep you from admitting your true condition. Pride masks the true condition of your heart. It keeps you from dealing with the truth. It distorts your vision. Pride hardens your heart, and as a result, you truly cannot see clearly.

You begin to view yourself as a victim. You hold back forgiveness, and you create barriers or walls of protection around you so that no one else can hurt you. We become focused on ourselves and the injustices.

This reduces or removes tenderness, and it creates a loss of sensitivity. We are then hindered in our ability to hear God's voice. This situation becomes a perfect scenario for the spirit of deception to operate.

Betrayal in a close relationship can be devastating. To betray someone is the ultimate abandonment of covenant. When betrayal occurs, the relationship cannot be restored unless genuine repentance follows. It happens all the time in our homes through divorce and splits in churches.

We must come to the place where we trust God and not ourselves.

The Key is to ACT – not react. The acts of forgiveness and release of the offense to the Lord are the first steps we must take.

I attended a meeting with a speaker from Ghana. His father was chief of a tribe and had many wives.

One of his father's wives had his mother killed. From that day on, he and his brothers and sisters lived in poverty; they were outcasts from his father.

As a young man, he gave his life to the Lord, and he became a preacher. He also thought he had forgiven his stepmother for killing his mother.

The Lord dealt with him on this matter. As a result, he approached his stepmother and told her that he forgave her. She immediately became emotional, and she asked him for forgiveness. She took Jesus in her heart, and she became saved. As a result of his obedience, all the wives and most of the children were eventually saved, and the whole tribe became Christian.

This testimony affected me greatly. Imagine, he forgave the person who killed his mother, and this man and his brothers and sisters lived their childhood in poverty because of their mother's death.

In the past, it had been easier for me to forgive a person rather than to confront them. However, the word states:

Matthew 18:15 NIV If your brother sins against you, go and show him his fault, just between the two of you. If he listens to you, you have won your brother over.

Matthew 5:44 NIV But I tell you: Love your enemies and pray for those who persecute you.

So, remember *James 4:7 NIV*. Submit yourselves, then, to God. Resist the devil, and he will flee from you.

We resist the devil by not becoming offended. We must stay obedient to God. Do what He tells us to do. It may be to go to the individual and ask for forgiveness. It may be to do nothing more than pray for the individual. Later, He may have you do something – like write a letter.

However, if you have offended someone, ask the Holy Spirit to lead you. Most likely He will tell you to go to them in love. Hold your tongue and let them speak. In humility, ask them to forgive you if you have offended them in any way. You may not agree with what they have to say. Explain to them that you will ask the Holy Spirit to reveal all hidden truths.

On another occasion, a couple in my church spoke negatively of my ministry. I wanted to speak to them, but they refused any contact with me. I continually asked God what to do. I kept praying for them and asking for all truths to come to the light.

Several months later during a church service, the Lord spoke to me. He said go the woman and ask her to forgive you for any way you have offended her. I said, "Lord, she will not speak to me." He said, "Haven't I told you to go to them seventy-seven times."

Matthew 18: 21-22 NIV Then Peter came to Jesus and asked, "Lord, how many times shall I forgive my brother when he sins against me? Up to seven times?" Jesus answered, "I tell you, not seven times, but seventy-seven times."

Eventually the wife spoke to me, and said, "Judy, the problem is not you. It is my husband. He has baggage to deal with and refuses to see and hear the truth." You see I was working with one of his children who needed to be set free.

The enemy has tried to bring back to me the hurts and wounds of the past, but I will not entertain those thoughts. I rebuke them, and I put them immediately out of my mind. It is history, and I need to live in the present.

Philippians 4:8 NIV Finally, brothers, whatever is true, whatever is noble, whatever is right, whatever is pure, whatever is lovely, whatever is admirable--if anything is excellent or praiseworthy--think about such things.

There are spiritual principles at work here: I asked for forgiveness, received forgiveness from God, forgave the other party, and was obedient to our Lord when He told me what to do. **The Keys are forgiveness and obedience.** I asked for forgiveness, I gave forgiveness. I listened, and I obeyed the leading of the Holy Spirit.

Love is the tool that keeps us free from the lies and darts of the enemy. We must put on the Armor of God daily (*Ephesians 6:12*). The importance of the shoes of the gospel of peace must never be forgotten. We must walk in peace with our fellow man. However, we are never to compromise the truths of God to walk in that peace. Remember, the keys are forgiveness and obedience.

Colossians 3:12-14 NIV Therefore as God's chosen people, holy and dearly loved, clothe yourselves with compassion, kindness, humility, gentleness, and patience. Bear with each other and forgive whatever grievances you may have against one another. Forgive as the Lord forgave you. And over all these virtues put on love, which binds them all together in perfect unity.

To forgive is a decision you must make. It has nothing to do with your emotions or "how you feel."

By being willing to forgive, God will honor that decision; he will help you remove the unforgiveness, resentment, and bitterness. All it takes is your "will" to be obedient to God.

Often unforgiveness, resentment, and bitterness can cause physical illnesses, i.e., arthritis, aches, and pains in our body.

Forgiveness Prayer

Heavenly Father,

Forgive me for harboring any unforgiveness, resentment, and bitterness. Please reveal to my mind those that I have offended or need to forgive.

Help me, Holy Spirit, to stay obedient to our Lord, and convict me of all my wrong doings so that I may walk closer to the light. Amen.

Please pray the following for those who you have offended, or you need to forgive.

Lord, forgive me for whatever I have done to _____ (name of person).

Lord, forgive _____ (name of person) for whatever they have done to me.

Lord, I forgive _____ (name of person).

Lord, forgive us for what we have both done to you.

I release _____ (name of person).

I declare and decree it is done!

Spirit of Rejection

Rejection is an act of denying love to someone. When we are rejected by others, we can also reject ourselves.

Rejection is a spirit. I believe that there are several other spirits that work closely with rejection to bring dysfunction into our lives and our families. Some of these are the strongman of lying spirits, and the spirit of heaviness.

How can it come into our lives? It can create bondage in our lives due to generational curses. These evil spirits may have entered your family bloodline many years ago. It could have happened because of someone denying family members love and affection. It could be a result of marrying dysfunctional people. It could be a result of alcoholism, divorce, abandonment, or a controlling relationship.

Some of the characteristics of a person having a spirit of rejection are the following:

> Sarcasm and ridicule
> Compulsively clean
> Perfectionism
> Anger and rage
> Eating disorder/self-mutilation
> Depression
> Suicide

Inwardly a person feeling rejected demonstrates shame, disgrace, embarrassment, regret, dishonor, humiliation, and condemnation. They feel that they are not wanted, not loved, not appreciated, and not good enough.

A person performs or strives to earn their acceptance. They believe that they are loved for what they do rather that for who they are.

The lying spirits continually reinforce their dysfunctional beliefs with spirits of deception, accusations, slander, gossip, and lies.

The spirit of heaviness brings in sorrow, self-pity, despair, hopelessness, broken hearted, depression, and suicidal tendencies.

Our spirit is the Holy Spirit within us. It is meant to influence our minds and emotions. The person with the spirit of rejection allows Satan and his evil spirits to control our minds and emotions. The enemy is continually at work to divide us from God, and to create disunity in our families.

God loves us and wants to take away our pain. But first, He wants us to understand how the enemy operates. There are evil spirits that can harass us and torment us daily. Their sole function is to kill, steal, and destroy God's people.

We must fight continually against the weapons of the enemy. We are all in continual warfare. We are not alone. Get a prayer partner and pray together daily. There is power in agreement.

We must target our prayers. Pray specific not general prayers. Learn the enemies' names and demand them to leave.

Let us first deal with the person who has caused you to feel rejected. You must forgive that person. The Lord knows how much that person has wounded you, but you must forgive.

Matthew 6:14-15 NIV For if you forgive men when they sin against you, your heavenly Father will also forgive you. But if you do not forgive men their sins, your Father will not forgive your sins.

Please pray the Forgiveness Prayer in the previous section.

Prayers for Rejection Issues

Prayer of Repentance for the Spirit of Self-Rejection

Heavenly Father,

I repent for rejecting myself. I repent for all the negative things I have thought and said about myself. I repent of not accepting myself, and for trying to be someone I was never meant to be. I repent for not believing that I have worth and value, just as I am.

I turn away from rejecting myself, and I renounce all the lies I have believed about myself. I renounce and break every curse I have thought or spoken about myself. I choose to accept myself. I break all soul-ties with self-rejection, heaviness, deception, lying spirits, and with every spirit that would lead me to reject myself.

Lord, I ask you to separate me from all generational curses and vows that have caused this spirit of rejection and other spirits associated with it to have an open door in my life. I demand that all the roots of rejection are destroyed, and that all the bloodline doors that have caused rejection are closed.

I cast the spirit of rejection off me, and I ask the Holy Spirit to fill me with his truth. Holy Spirit, please come and fill all the void places within me. I decree and declare it is done! Amen.

Prayer of Repentance for the Fear of Rejection

Heavenly Father,

I repent for giving into the fear of rejection. I repent of all lying, deception, suspicion, and mistrust, control, or manipulation that either I have given place to or my family.

Lord, I repent of trying to please people instead of you. I repent of my self-protective behavior and all self-pity. And now, I renounce the fear of rejection and all my destructive behavior.

I renounce and break all soul-ties and generational ties to the fear of rejection, and I break its hold on my life. I refuse to be bound to this fear any longer, and I break down this wall of fear of rejection. I break it down now, in Jesus' mighty name. Lord, I ask you to shut all my bloodline doors that have been opened due to fear of rejection. I declare and decree that it is done! Amen.

Prayer for Repentance for Rejecting God

Heavenly Father,

I am sorry for all the times and all the ways I have rejected you. Please forgive me.

I repent for not believing you, for not listening to you, and for refusing your love. I repent for not trusting you, and for doubting your love for me.

I repent for all the stubbornness, pride, self-will, and rebellion that I have walked in.

In the name of Jesus, I renounce all rejection of God. I renounce all involvement with any spirit that would lead me to reject God.

I renounce and break all vows and covenants, all soul-ties and generational ties that would bind me to the rejection of God. Lord, I ask you to shut all my bloodline doors that have been opened due to rejecting you.

I choose to love God with all my heart, with all my soul and with my entire mind. I declare and decree that it is done! Amen. Some of these prayers are found in Chris Hayward's book, ***The End of Rejection.***

Setting your Boundaries

Because God gave dominion over the earth to man, the only way God can intervene in the life of any one on earth is if they give Him dominion over their life.

God gave Adam and Eve boundaries in the Garden of Eden. He told them to eat of every tree except the tree of knowledge of good and evil.

Boundaries are essential to a healthy, balanced life. Boundaries are simply defined as who you are and who you are not. They state your goals and the purposes for your life.

Boundaries then safeguard your goals and purposes. They say where you end, and another person starts.

They are like property lines. Others can do what they want on their property, but not on yours. Once you set your boundaries, no one gets to redefine these parameters except you and the Lord.

There are many types of boundaries:

>personal boundaries,
>physical boundaries,
>emotional boundaries,
>spiritual boundaries,
>sexual boundaries.

We must spend time with our Lord. Listen to Him and ask Him to help you define who you are.

First, you must know that you are loved which is essential to all relationships and activities. You must realize that you are a child of God, and that He loves you. Are you secure in knowing who you are? He knows every hair on your head.

Your priorities in life are:

1. God first
2. Yourself
3. Your family
4. What God has called you to do.

When you put yourself as a priority after God, you have started developing correct boundaries.

According to Bill Guiltier, author of ***Jesus Set Boundaries***, Jesus had limitations. He knew he needed nourishment, rest, and could only be in one place at a time.

He had personal needs that took priority in his life. Sometimes those needs took priority over others.

He did not feel guilty because he knew He had to spend time with God, which gave him focus and energy. So, he was never in danger of burn-out, being angry, or depressed.

Jesus said "no" to inappropriate behaviors of others. He said "no" to control, manipulation, abuse, pride of others, and cynicism. He spoke truth in love to those who were misguided.

Often, he did not do what people wanted him to do. There were many people he did not help. And whenever he did help other people, he expected them to do their part.

Guidelines for setting boundaries:

1. Have personal prayer time.
2. Be honest and direct.

Matthew 5:37 Simply, let your yes be yes, and your no, no; anything beyond this comes from the evil one.

3. Set priorities.
4. Please God and not people.
5. Obey God.

Boundaries impact all our lives. We have the responsibility of creating and enforcing our own boundaries. You must be aware of your limitations.

Our physical boundaries must be created so that we know our limitations so we will be safe and appropriate.

Physical boundaries refer to our bodies. It is our ability to control when and how others approach us, see us, or touch us.

This boundary separates us from others. It stops with our skin.

Examples: refusing a hug, locking a door on your bedroom, closing a curtain, building a fence between your home and your neighbor's property.

According to Anne Katherine, author of ***Boundaries, Where You End and I Begin***, Empowerment is the answer. If your physical and sexual boundaries have been violated in the past, you were a victim then, but you do not have to be a victim any longer.

As of this moment, know that you have the right to determine how your body is treated. Even a light touch can be removed if you do not want it. Simply take his hand off your shoulder and say, "No thank you."

Move away and say, "I do not like that." Or say, "Please ask permission before you touch me again." We do not have to be courteous when someone is rude or aggressive. Say, "Touch me again, and I will scream. I will embarrass you in front of everyone." When you protect yourself, you empower yourself.

Our emotional boundaries are our feelings and reactions. We each have our own set of emotional boundaries, and they are individually distinctive.

They will help us disengage with manipulative and controlling emotions of others. We respond to the world based on our values, beliefs, goals, and concerns. When your emotional boundaries are well-developed, you are in charge of your own feelings, moods, and problems.

You can be compassionate toward others without taking on their feelings or problems and making them your own. Our emotional health is related to the health of our boundaries.

Another sign of emotional boundaries is learning to take responsibility for ourselves. This may mean at times we must confront inappropriate behavior. We may have to back off helping someone and direct them to someone else.

Boundaries can be spoken or unspoken. Walking away from a person who is insulting you speak as loudly as your words. I set limits on what people say about me. When you let someone verbally abuse you or hurt you, you have not protected your personal boundaries. Do not let them cross the line.

Setting a boundary means you respect yourself. When you respect yourself, you protect yourself from inappropriate behavior.

Spiritual boundaries help us to distinguish God's will from our own.

Matthew 6:33 NIV But seek first his kingdom and his righteousness, and all these things will be given to you.

Through God, we will find peace, contentment, and right thinking. We instinctively will know who we can talk to about our spiritual beliefs and who we cannot.

Mental/Intellectual boundaries give us the freedom to have our own thoughts and opinions.

Sexual boundaries are the choices we make as to who we interact with sexually and to what extent. You know what is safe and appropriate.

Remember the purpose of setting boundaries is to take care of you, not to create walls. Say no to obligations that make you miserable. Protect your health. By saying, "no" to more things, you will then have the time, energy, and resources to get really good at the things you want to say "yes" to.

Boundaries should be clear, specific, reasonable, and enforceable. An example is telling your son that you will buy him a car, but he must pay for his own car insurance, maintenance, and fuel.

I want to tell you a personal example. I was with a group of ministry people, and we were to visit a very large ministry in downtown Washington, DC.

They were in the middle of a large project that was extremely time-consuming. The individual who was showing us around the organization started demanding that we all help them.

She confronted each one of us individually. The other people in my group said that they would do something. I said "no", and that was it. When we got back to our van, some of the people said, "Judy, you had the courage to say 'no'." They had wished they had done so.

Another example, my son and I were going to visit my family that we had not seen for several years. I want to let you know that my mother had a serious control problem.

We arrived at our destination by plane and were taken to my sister's home to refresh ourselves. We had decided that we would then go to see our mother.

Upon arriving at her home, I went up to the door. She started to yell at me for not getting there sooner. She had not seen her grandson in four years, and all she did was get us upset.

So, I said to everyone, "Get back in the car, we are leaving here." I believe that was my first experience in really setting my boundaries. I was proud of myself, and I knew from then on, I was going to have healthy boundaries.

With good boundaries, we can have the wonderful assurance that comes from knowing we can and will protect ourselves from the ignorance, meanness, or thoughtlessness of others.

According to Anne Katherine, "We learn about our boundaries by the way we are treated as children. Then we teach others where our boundaries are by the way we let them treat us."

Most people will respect our boundaries if we indicate where they are. With some people, however, we must actively defend them.

In healthy relationships, people respect each other's boundaries. Each person respects the needs, values, thoughts, and feelings of the other, regardless how they differ from their own.

When respect is reciprocal, the self-worth of both people will probably increase. Without boundaries, you will limit God's plan for you. You must set limits to live the life God has planned for you.

I do recommend you reading the following book by Anne Katherine, **Where You End and I Begin**,

Prayer for Establishing Healthy Boundaries

Heavenly Father,

I repent for not setting up healthy boundaries. Growing up I was surrounded by dysfunctional people who constantly crossed my boundary lines. As you know, I did not have healthy relationships. Lord, I ask you to shut all my bloodline doors that have been opened due to unhealthy boundaries that were established in my life.

Lord, please help me with establishing healthy boundaries which includes physical, emotional, personal, spiritual, and sexual boundaries.

I surrender this dysfunctional area of my life to you. I ask for your wisdom, revelation, and insights. Also, Lord, I need boldness and courage.

Thank you, Lord, for molding and remaking me in your image. I declare and decree that it is done! Amen.

Warfare Prayers

Everyday Prayers

Prayer for Casting off Anything That Has Come Upon You

In the name of Jesus, I speak to all demonic spirits including tormenting spirit and harassing spirits. I rebuke you, and demand that you get off me by the power of the Holy name of our Lord Jesus Christ. Go to the arid places never to return. I declare and decree that it is done! Amen.

Word Curses Prayer

By the authority and power given to me by the holy name of our Lord, Jesus Christ, I demand these word curses, assignments, judgments, and spirits of witchcraft, jealousy, envy, strife, and every scheme and plan of the enemy to be broken and shattered.

I demand that all strongmen and demonic spirits that are associated with these curses to leave me now and go to the arid places. I ask the Lord to send blessings and conviction to the originator. I decree and declare it is done! Amen.

Prayer for Cleansing Your Home

This prayer is not a deep cleansing of your home and property. There are instructions in my other books for a thorough cleansing. After a thorough cleansing, this prayer should be used daily. Just walk through your home and pray out loud.

In the name of Jesus, I demand that all demonic spirits to get off me (also other family members and pets) and out of my home and off this property.

You cannot attach yourself to anyone or anything. Go in the name of or our Lord, Jesus Christ. Lord, please release your angel armies to keep my home and family safe. I declare and decree that it is done!

Open the front door and tell them to leave. Then ask the Holy Spirit to come and fill your home.

Books & References

Generational Curses

1. ***Merriam-Webster's Collegiate Dictionary*** 1994-1995

2. Rebecca Brown, M.D., ***Unbroken Curses***, (New Kensington, PA: Whitaker House, 1995)

3. Judy Farris-Smith, ***Targeted Prayers***, (Copyright @ 2020 by Little Sparrow Ministries, Lindale, Texas)

4. Wikipedia, the free encyclopedia, en.wikipedia.org, ***Slavery, Treatment of Slaves in US***

5. Britannica Online Encyclopedia, Britannica.com, ***Slavery***

6. Michael A. Hoffman, II, ***They Were White, and They were Slaves***, 1993

7. Robert C. Davis, ***Christian Slaves, Muslim Masters***, 2003 Palgrave Macmillan, NY, NY

8. Oscar Handlin, ***The Truth About Slavery***, April 21, 1993

Ungodly Soul-Ties

1. Bill and Sue Banks, ***Breaking Unhealthy Soul-ties*** (Kirkwood, MO: Impact Christian Books, Inc.1999, 2001)

2. Judy Farris-Smith, ***Targeted Prayers***, (Copyright @ 2020 by Little Sparrow Ministries, Lindale, Texas)

Word Curses/Judgments/ Spoken Word

1. Charles Capps**, *The Tongue – A Creative Force,*** (Tulsa, OK: Harrison House, Inc 1995)

2. Francis Frangipane, ***Three Battlegrounds*** (Cedar Rapids, IA: Advancing Church Publications, 1989)

3. ***The World Book Dictionary*** 1981 Edition (Copyright @ 1981 by Doubleday & Company, Inc.)

4. Judy Farris-Smith, ***Targeted Prayers***, (Copyright @ 2020 by Little Sparrow Ministries, Lindale, Texas)

Spirit of Offense

1. Judy Farris-Smith, ***Targeted Prayers***, (Copyright @ 2020 by Little Sparrow Ministries, Lindale, Texas)

Spirit of Rejection

1. Chris Hayward, ***The End of Rejection,*** (Ventura, CA: Copyright @ 2007 by Regal Books)

2. Sermoncentral.com

3. Judy H Farris-Smith, ***Setting Yourself Free, Deliverance from Darkness,*** Copyright @ 2020 by Little Sparrow Ministries, Lindale, Texas)

Setting Your Boundaries

1. Anne Katherine MA, **_Where You End and I Begin_**, (Copyright @ 1991 Parkside Publishing Corporation, Park Ridge, Illinois 60068)

2. www.make-my-life-work.com
   Jesus Set Boundaries

3. www.soulshepherding.org

4. I Am Global Church

Warfare Prayers

1. Judy H Farris-Smith, **_Setting Yourself Free, Deliverance from Darkness,_** Copyright @ 2020 Little Sparrow Ministries, Lindale, Texas

Other Books by Little Sparrow Ministries

Can be ordered on littlesparrowministries.com

Little Sparrow Ministries, ***Setting Yourself Free, Deliverance from Darkness*** (Little Sparrow Ministries, Copyright © 2020 Lindale, Texas 75771)

Little Sparrow Ministries, ***Targeted Prayers*** (Little Sparrow Ministries, Copyright © 2020, Lindale, Texas 75771)

Little Sparrow Ministries, ***Set Yourself Free Little Children and Come to Me*** (Little Sparrow Ministries, Copyright © 2017 Lindale, Texas 75771)

Little Sparrow Ministries, ***Truth vs. Lies, Information for Teenagers*** (Little Sparrow Ministries, Copyright © 2017 Lindale, Texas 75771)

Little Sparrow Ministries, *He is in your Fire, PTSD Workbook.* (Little Sparrow Ministries, Copyright © 2017 Lindale, Texas 75771)

Little Sparrow Ministries, *Little Bit, the Miracle Kid*, (Little Sparrow Ministries, Copyright © 2009 Lindale, Texas 75771)

Little Sparrow Ministries, *Have Faith, Inspirational Testimonies* (Little Sparrow Ministries, Copyright © 2011 Lindale, Texas 75771

Little Sparrow Ministries, *Victim to Victory* (Little Sparrow Ministries, Copyright © 2017 Lindale, Texas 75771)

www.ingramcontent.com/pod-product-compliance
Lightning Source LLC
LaVergne TN
LVHW011731060526
838200LV00051B/3120